Look, Listen, Taste, Touch, and Smell

LEARNING ABOUT YOUR FIVE SENSES

WRITTEN BY PAMELA HILL NETTLETON
ILLUSTRATED BY BECKY SHIPE

Thanks to our advisers for their expertise, research, and advice:
Angela Busch, M.D., All About Children Pediatrics, Minneapolis, Minnesota

Susan Kesselring, M.A., Literacy Educator
Rosemount-Apple Valley-Eagan (Minnesota) School District

PICTURE WINDOW BOOKS
MINNEAPOLIS, MINNESOTA

Managing Editor: Bob Temple
Creative Director: Terri Foley
Editor: Kristin Thoennes Keller
Editorial Adviser: Andrea Cascardi
Copy Editor: Laurie Kahn
Designer: Melissa Voda
Page production: The Design Lab
The illustrations in this book were rendered digitally.

Picture Window Books
5115 Excelsior Boulevard
Suite 232
Minneapolis, MN 55416
1-877-845-8392
www.picturewindowbooks.com

Printed in the United States of America.

Library of Congress Cataloging-in-Publication Data
Nettleton, Pamela Hill.
  Look, listen, taste, touch, and smell: learning about your five senses /
by Pamela Hill Nettleton ; illustrated by Becky Shipe.
    p. cm. — (The amazing body)
Summary: An introduction to the five senses and the organs that perform
the functions of sight, hearing, smell, taste and touch. Includes
bibliographical references and index.
  ISBN 1-4048-0257-6 (lib. bdg.)
1. Senses and sensation—Juvenile literature. [1. Senses and sensation.]
I. Shipe, Becky, 1977– ill. II. Title.
  QP434 .N48 2004
  612.8—dc22   2003018188

Do you ever roast marshmallows? You hear the crackle of the fire. You smell the smoke. You feel the warmth. You see the marshmallows turning golden brown. And finally you can taste the yummy treat. Your five senses help you enjoy what you do!

You have five senses that tell you what is going on around you. They are hearing, sight, smell, taste, and touch.

Your senses help you know if you are safe or in danger. You also use your senses for fun.

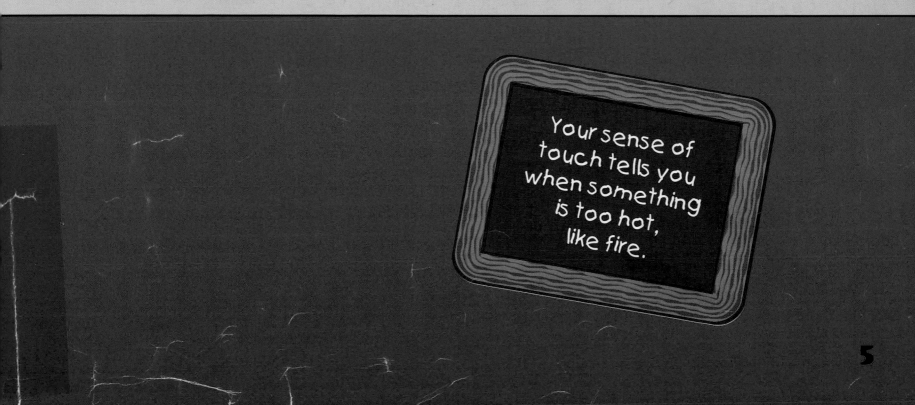

Your sense of touch tells you when something is too hot, like fire.

Each of your senses has a special place on your body. Your ears hear. Your eyes see. Your nose smells. Your tongue tastes. Your skin touches.

Each of these places sends signals to your brain.
Your brain understands these signals. It knows
whether you hear music or someone talking.
It knows whether you smell something good
or something stinky.

Getting a good night's sleep helps keep your senses sharp.

The part of your ear on the outside of your head catches the sounds around you. Then sound moves inside your head.

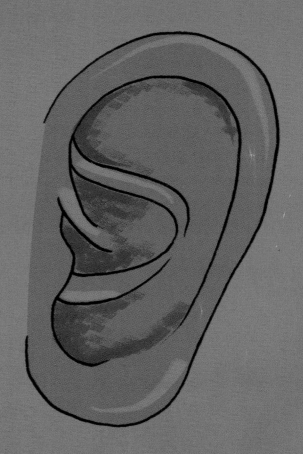

Earwax looks and feels gross, but it helps your ears. It catches germs and dirt before they can get inside your ear.

Your ear has many other parts inside that you can't see. These parts turn noises into signals your brain can understand.

The colored part of your eye is called the iris. The black hole in the center of the iris is called the pupil. The pupil lets in light for your eye to see.

Glasses can help you see better when the inside parts of your eyes don't work so well.

Behind your eye is an optic nerve. It takes the pictures your eye sees and sends them to the brain. Your eyes know how to focus, like a camera.

11

Sure, your nose helps you breathe. But it also sniffs for smells. A special place inside your nose helps tell one smell from another.

Kids can smell more things than grown-ups.

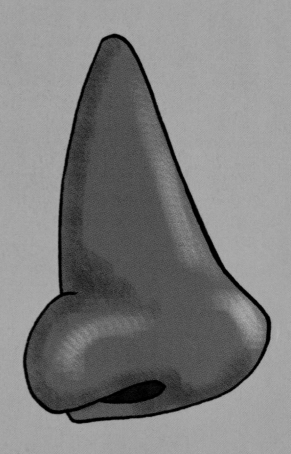

Your nose sends signals to your brain so you know when to say, "Yum! What's in the oven?"

Your nose and your tongue work together
to help you taste. Your nose tells your brain
what food smells like. Your tongue is covered
with bumpy taste buds.

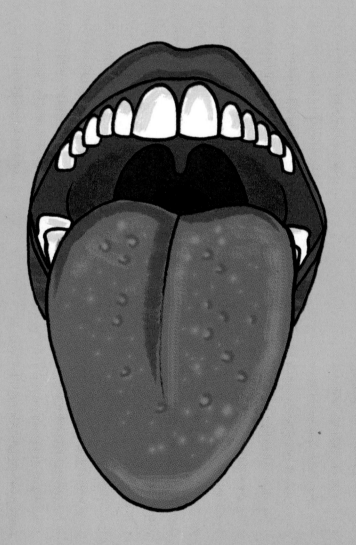

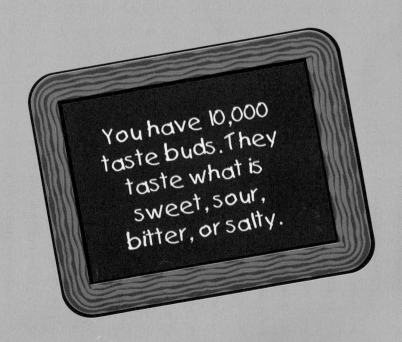

You have 10,000 taste buds. They taste what is sweet, sour, bitter, or salty.

The taste buds tell your brain whether you are eating pizza or pickles.

You touch most things with your fingers.
But your skin is always touching something—
your clothes, the cool air, your desk seat.

Your skin has three layers. The top layer makes new skin cells. This means your skin will never wear out.

Your skin tells you if something is soft or hard, fuzzy or smooth. Your skin tells you if you are hot or cold. Your skin sends messages to your brain: *Hey! Put on a jacket!*

A special doctor who takes care of your
ears, nose, and throat is called an ENT.
ENT stands for ear, nose, and throat.
An eye doctor checks your eyes
and helps you get glasses.

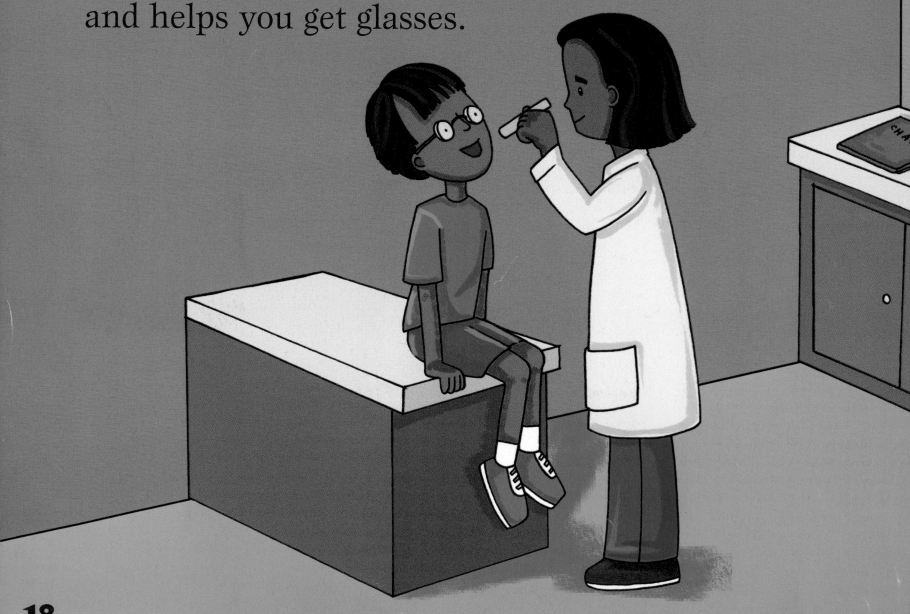

There are doctors who take care of your skin.
And if your senses have trouble talking
to your brain, you go to a special doctor
called a neurologist.

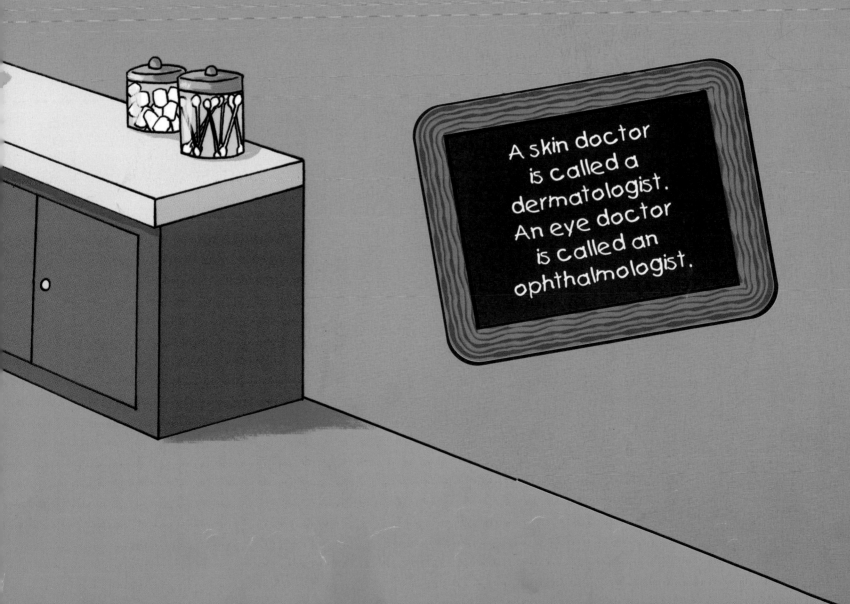

A skin doctor
is called a
dermatologist.
An eye doctor
is called an
ophthalmologist.

Keep your senses sharp. Wear earplugs around loud noises. Wear goggles or a mask for hockey and snowboarding.

Never put anything in your nose, ears, or eyes.

Wear sunglasses in bright light. Wear sunscreen, and wash your skin with soap and water. Protect your senses!

YOUR FIVE SENSES

See these people? Their senses are very busy in this picture. Make a list of ways that you see people using their senses. Compare your list with a friend.

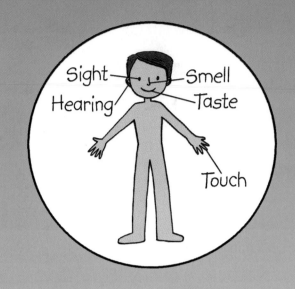

TAKE A TASTE TEST!

Prove that your nose and your tongue work together to help you taste. Plug your nose, and take a bite of a warm chocolate-chip cookie. Now, unplug your nose, and take another bite. Does the cookie taste better the first or second time?

TOOLS OF THE TRADE

An eye doctor uses special tools called scopes to look into your eyes. The scopes make the inside of your eyes look big. This helps the doctor see if your eyes are healthy inside.

An ENT also uses a scope with a light. He or she looks up your nose, in your throat, and in your ears to see if those areas are healthy.

GLOSSARY

brain (BRAYN)—the organ inside your head that controls your movements, thoughts, and feelings

neurologist (noo-RAW-luh-jist)—a doctor who studies and treats problems with the nervous system

senses (SENSS-uhz)—the five powers we use to learn about our surroundings

signal (SIG-nuhl)—a message between our brains and our senses

skin (SKIN)—the outer covering of humans and animals

TO LEARN MORE

At the Library

Aliki. *My Five Senses*. New York: HarperCollins, 1991.

Cole, Joanna. *You Can't Smell a Flower with Your Ear: All About Your 5 Senses*. New York: Grosset & Dunlap, 1994.

Ziefert, Harriet. *You Can't Taste a Pickle with Your Ear: A Book About Your 5 Senses*. Brooklyn: Blue Apple Books, 2002.

On the Web

Fact Hound offers a safe, fun way to find Web sites related to this book. All of the sites on Fact Hound have been researched by our staff.

http://www.facthound.com

1. Visit the Fact Hound home page.
2. Enter a search word related to this book, or type in this special code: 1404802576.
3. Click the FETCH IT button.

Your trusty Fact Hound will fetch the best sites for you!

INDEX

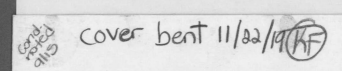